Lost at Windy River

A TRUE STORY OF SURVIVAL

Trina Rathgeber

ILLUSTRATED BY
Alina Pete

COLORED BY
Jillian Dolan

ORCA BOOK PUBLISHERS

Published in Canada and the United States in 2024 by Orca Book Publishers.
orcabook.com

Library and Archives Canada Cataloguing in Publication
Title: Lost at Windy River : a true story of survival / Trina Rathgeber ;
illustrated by Alina Pete ; coloured by Jillian Dolan.
Names: Rathgeber, Trina, author. | Pete, Alina, artist. | Dolan, Jillian, colourist.
Identifiers: Canadiana (print) 2023058358X | Canadiana (ebook) 20230583652 |
ISBN 9781459832268 (softcover) | ISBN 9781459832275 (PDF)
Subjects: LCSH: Wilderness survival—Canada, Northern—Comic books, strips, etc. |
LCSH: Wilderness survival—Canada, Northern—Juvenile literature. |
CSH: Indigenous girls—Canada, Northern—Comic books, strips, etc. |
CSH: Indigenous girls—Canada, Northern—Juvenile literature. | LCGFT: Nonfiction comics.
Classification: LCC GV200.5 .R38 2024 | DDC j613.6/909719022—dc23

Library of Congress Control Number: 2023949566

Summary: This graphic novel for middle-grade readers tells the true story of how a young Indigenous girl survived nine days after getting lost during a snowstorm in northern Canada.

Orca Book Publishers is committed to reducing the consumption of nonrenewable resources in the production of our books. We make every effort to use materials that support a sustainable future.

Orca Book Publishers gratefully acknowledges the support for its publishing programs provided by the following agencies: the Government of Canada, the Canada Council for the Arts and the Province of British Columbia through the BC Arts Council and the Book Publishing Tax Credit.

Cover and interior artwork by Alina Pete.
Cover and interior color by Jillian Dolan.
Design by Dahlia Yuen.
Edited by Kirstie Hudson.

Printed and bound in South Korea.

27 26 25 24 • 1 2 3 4

This book is dedicated to my grandma Ilse
and all her grandchildren.

Ilse visiting Nueltin Lake on
a trip with her husband Brian.

Ilse and her
grandson Owen.

Photos courtesy of Ilse Schweder and Trina Rathgeber.

Preface

In 1952 Canadian author Farley Mowat published a book called *People of the Deer*. One of the chapters was inspired by my grandmother's story of survival in the north. She always felt strongly that it was her story to tell, not his. She shared it with my family, and now I'm going to share it with you.

Chapter One: North of '53

I'm off to a school to talk about my old story that everyone is so curious about.

All right. Enjoy spending time with the children.

For the birds?

Yes, of course! Got to feed the birds—and the squirrels too.

After all these years, people are still talking about those books he wrote.

1

Ilse was often in schools, teaching beadwork, traditional weaving on a loom and moccasin making,

and, of course, once in a while she'd be asked to tell "her story."

Hello.

Oh, hello, Ilse. Please come in. We have a chair for you here.

Students, please make your way to our story area and find a seat. Make room for everyone.

WELCOME!!
SPECIAL GUEST
ILSE
SCHWEDER

DEER
RABBIT
WOLF

We are honored to have Ilse Schweder join us today. It's rare to read a book and then meet one of its real-life characters.

I encourage you to listen closely and take this opportunity to ask questions of the real "Stella."

A **tobacco tie** is a bundle of tobacco wrapped with cloth and twine. It is offered when a request is respectfully made to an Elder. If the Elder accepts the gift, it means they will support you with your ask.

Yes, you there.

Um, what was it like to be Stella?

She'd been here before, answering questions about Stella, thinking how the story the kids had read wasn't exactly what had happened.

How Farley Mowat had taken her story— *her* story—and made it his own.

How Stella's journey hadn't exactly been like hers.

Without an understanding of traditional knowledge and the land, how could he know what it took for her to survive?

She examined the string of tiny flowers on the ring she had beaded, each made up of five colored beads.

She was reminded of her capability and resourcefulness.

I'm not Stella, so I don't know what it's like to be her.

iskwêw pithîsiw nitisithihkâson. My Cree name is *Lady of the Thunderbird.*

I was born Ilse Schweder to Fred Schweder and Rosa Bighetty.

That character Stella couldn't have done what I did. She didn't know enough.

Me, however, I suppose I did.

Do you want to hear what really happened?

YES!!

All right then.

This is my story.

3

GROUNDHOG HILL

KAZAN RIVER

WOLF CAMP

GOOSE CAMP

SAND HILL CAMP

NORTH CAMP

SKELETON LAKE

HOME

KAZAN CAMP

SPRUCE CAMP

GEORGE!

LOON LAKE

WINDY RIVER

Ilse loved to be with her family. Just four years earlier her mother had died. Two years after that, Ilse and her two sisters had been taken to residential school.

Her older sister passed away there and never made it home. Her father then brought all the kids north to live together at the Windy River Trading Post.

Fred

Emigrated from Germany

Fur trader

Strong and strict

Clever

Resourceful

Tough

Expert sled-dog trainer

Charles

Oldest son

Respected northern guide to explorers

Mapmaker

Fur trader and trapper

Sled-dog trainer

Freddy

Skilled trapper and trader

Expert dog-team driver

Hunter and fisher

Ilse

Outdoorswoman

Connected with nature

Quick-witted and practical

Mary

Expert animal skinner

Food preserver

Strong fisher

Norman & Mike

Little brothers

Caring and sweet

Eager to learn

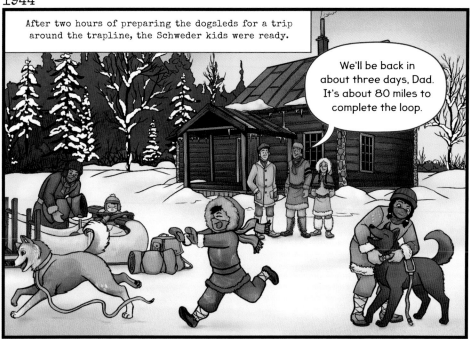

After two hours of preparing the dogsleds for a trip around the trapline, the Schweder kids were ready.

We'll be back in about three days, Dad. It's about 80 miles to complete the loop.

Ilse's coming to train the small dogs, and she's a great helper on the trapline.

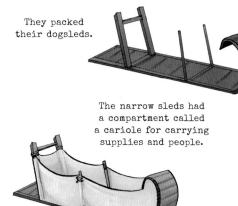

They packed their dogsleds.

The narrow sleds had a compartment called a cariole for carrying supplies and people.

All set?

Yes, Dad!

Wait!

I forgot something!

BRR!!

BRR!!

Okay, good to go!

Okay then. Goodbye, my dear.

Bye, Dad! Bye, Mary!

MUSH! MUSH!

The Windy Post was the northernmost post owned by the Revillon Frères fur company, which was later absorbed by the Hudson's Bay Company (HBC). After Fred's employment ended with the HBC, he and Charles and Freddy constructed a new post at the mouth of Windy River. They traded with the Inuit, Chipewyan and Cree.

Ilse concentrated on not falling behind. Her small dogs barked with excitement as they glided across the snow. It wouldn't be bright and sunny for long, as northern winter days are short.

In the summer the sisters spent time near George, picking blueberries and playing games. One day they gave him a moss wig and a name.

A **caribou boundary** is a human-made pile of stones used to help direct herds of caribou where hunters want them to go. George is a stone man, a pile of stones that resembles a human. It's another clever hunting tactic that would cause the animals to pause, giving hunters the opportunity to take aim and shoot.

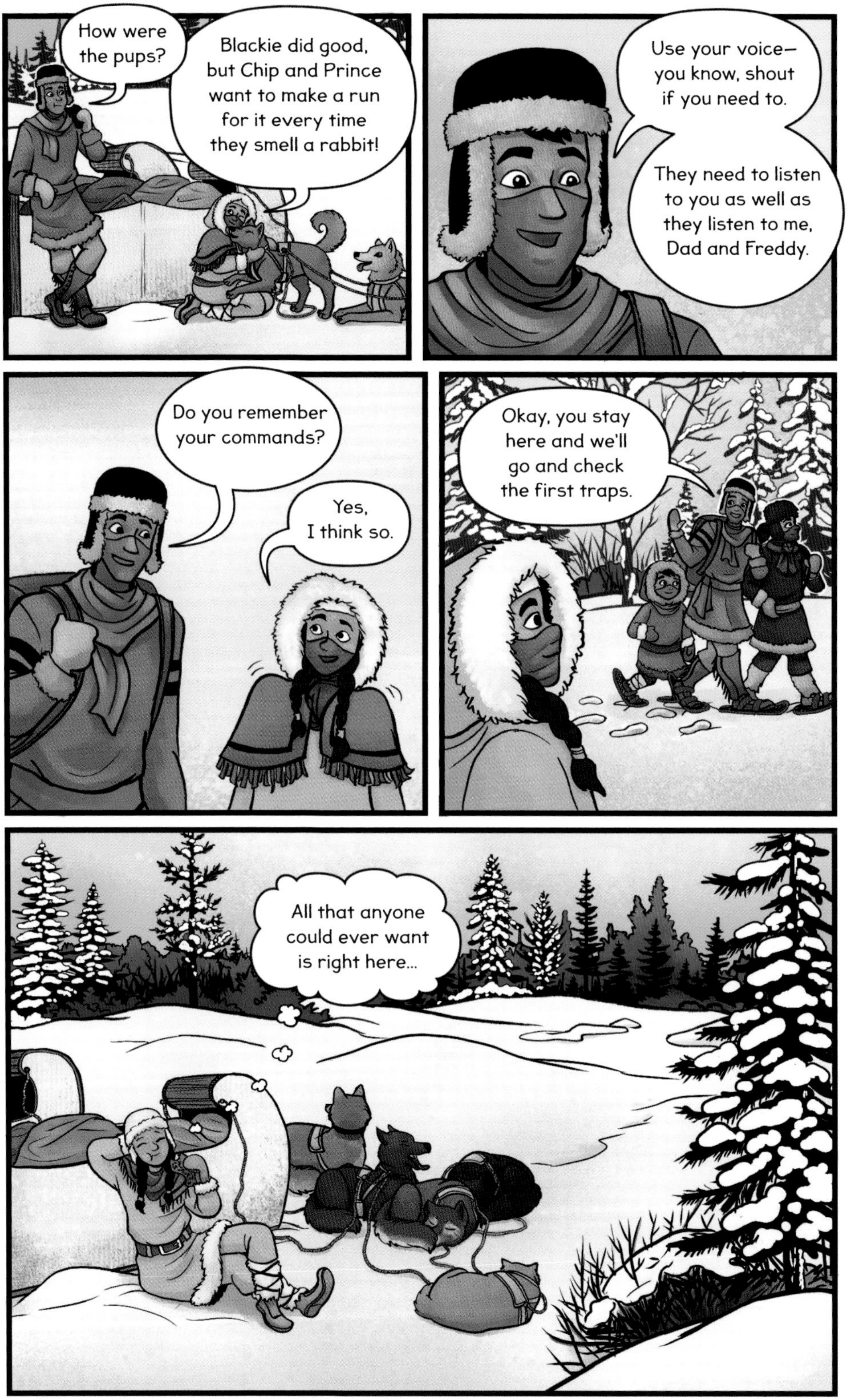

How were the pups?
Blackie did good, but Chip and Prince want to make a run for it every time they smell a rabbit!
Use your voice—you know, shout if you need to.
They need to listen to you as well as they listen to me, Dad and Freddy.
Do you remember your commands?
Yes, I think so.
Okay, you stay here and we'll go and check the first traps.
All that anyone could ever want is right here...

Ilse loved the north and daydreamed about when she had first moved here with her father after her mother passed and the farm near Winnipeg was sold.

Ilse remembered the feeling of peace as every mile they traveled north put her farther away from residential school.

That three-toed wolverine got one of the foxes.

It's ruined.

Is he still a problem?

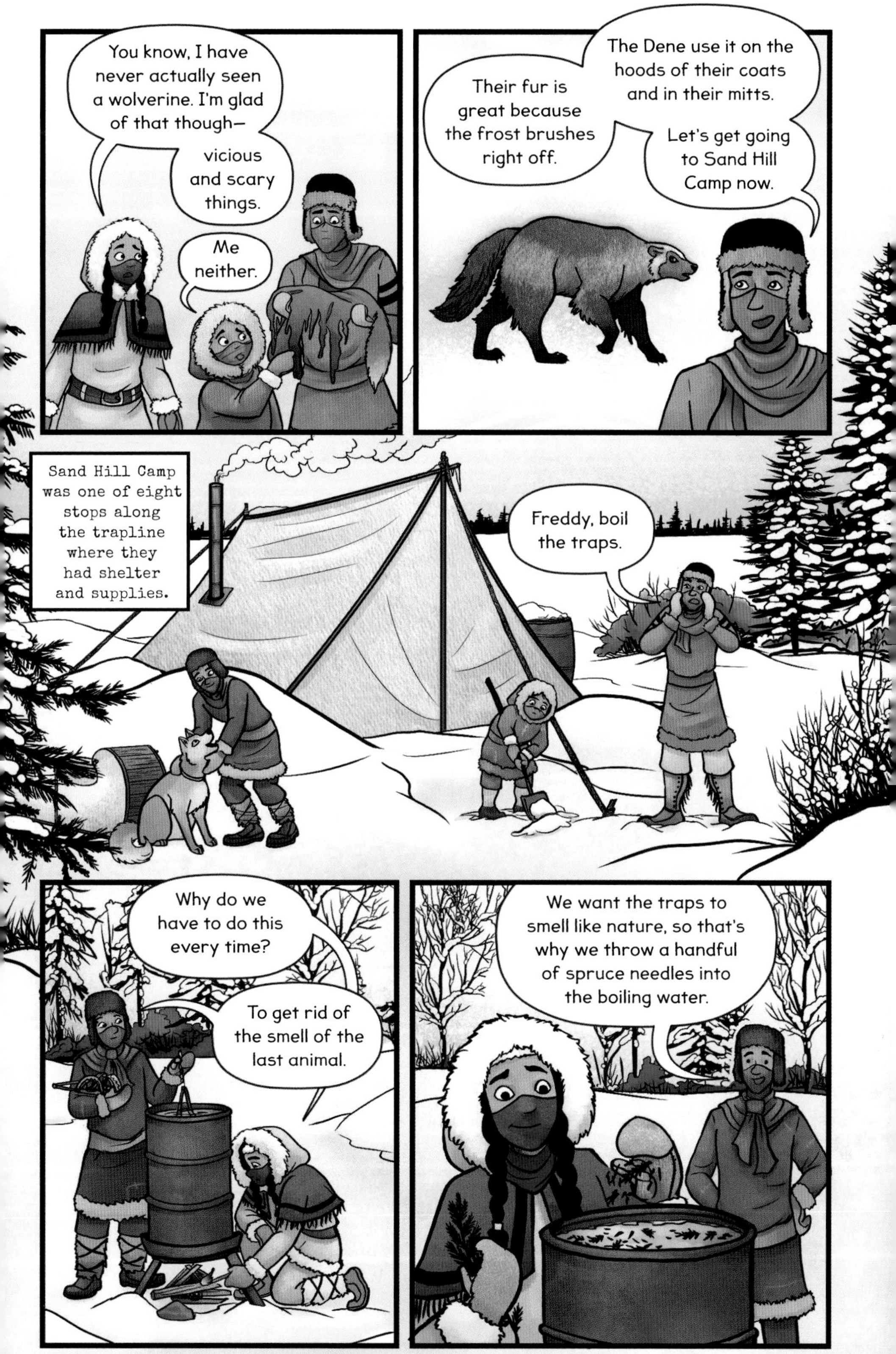
You know, I have never actually seen a wolverine. I'm glad of that though—
vicious and scary things.
Me neither.
Their fur is great because the frost brushes right off.
The Dene use it on the hoods of their coats and in their mitts.
Let's get going to Sand Hill Camp now.
Sand Hill Camp was one of eight stops along the trapline where they had shelter and supplies.
Freddy, boil the traps.
Why do we have to do this every time?
To get rid of the smell of the last animal.
We want the traps to smell like nature, so that's why we throw a handful of spruce needles into the boiling water.

Chapter Three: A Night at Camp

All right, time to turn in.

Tell us a story, Freddy!

The mimikwisiw are small dwarflike people.

Some people say they have no noses, while others say they surely have noses, just flat ones.

They are a bit hairy and dress themselves in leather clothes decorated with porcupine quills.

They are usually only seen by medicine people or children.

They are medicine people themselves, spirits of the water but also tricksters.

In one story two children ventured down to the river with gifts for the mimikwisiw.

Their mother was ill, and they wanted to trade their gifts for medicine.

They left a doll and some tobacco wrapped in birch bark.

The next morning they returned to find a bundle of plants rolled in the birch bark.

The two children ran home. Their grandmother told them to boil the plants into a tea for their mother.

When she drank it, she became sick, which caused her to empty the contents of her stomach, and she recovered the very next day.

So keep your eyes open, kids, and you just might see a mimikwisiw one day.

Good night now.

I've seen them in the cabin at Windy.

Running around the ledge.

Snooping!

Now off to sleep with you.

The next morning...

Go fill the pot with snow, Ilse.

Make sure it's white and fluffy.

No yellow!

I KNOW that!

Hot tea with sugar, bannock and beans on the menu.

Beans only for today. You can't travel with cans for very long or they will freeze and pop.

Dad learned that the hard way his first winter in the north.

The wind is picking up, Freddy, and see how the clouds are gray and low across the horizon?

There's a big storm coming. I'm sure of it.

I'll carry on to the trapline camp at Kazan River on my own.

The rest of you stay here until the storm passes.

Finish your chores and then go home.

Charles left them with the tasks of making him extra dog food for the trip home and mending areas of the shelter.

The small children begged Freddy to take them home right away...

...back to the comforts, the warmth and the radio programs.

A few hours later...

Gone home to Windy. Left on Thursday —Freddy

What's so funny?

We're laughing about the time Mary made herself a caribou-hide snowsuit. She didn't work the hide enough.

Yes, so when she went outside it froze stiff, and she fell over and couldn't get up!

Ilse and Norman, you'll drive this sled.

I took all the supplies, so this one is nice and light for the little dogs.

Now let's go. If we travel quickly, we should make it home before the storm hits.

They started their journey home across the tundra.

The tundra is an extremely cold and windy area that covers a large section of northern Canada. The winter days are short, and below the surface of the ground there is a permanent layer of frozen soil called **permafrost**. The area is nicknamed Land of the Little Sticks because the trees are small and skinny.

Ilse, try to keep up!

I'll take Norman so we can lighten your load even more.

Okay, but it's hard to see, and it's getting dark so fast too.

The storm was fierce. The wind whipped their faces— it was a complete whiteout. Ilse's dogs pulled this way and that. Freddy's more experienced dogs could likely make it home, even in bad weather.

Here. I'll tie the rope to your sled so we can stay together.

It's working, thank goodness.

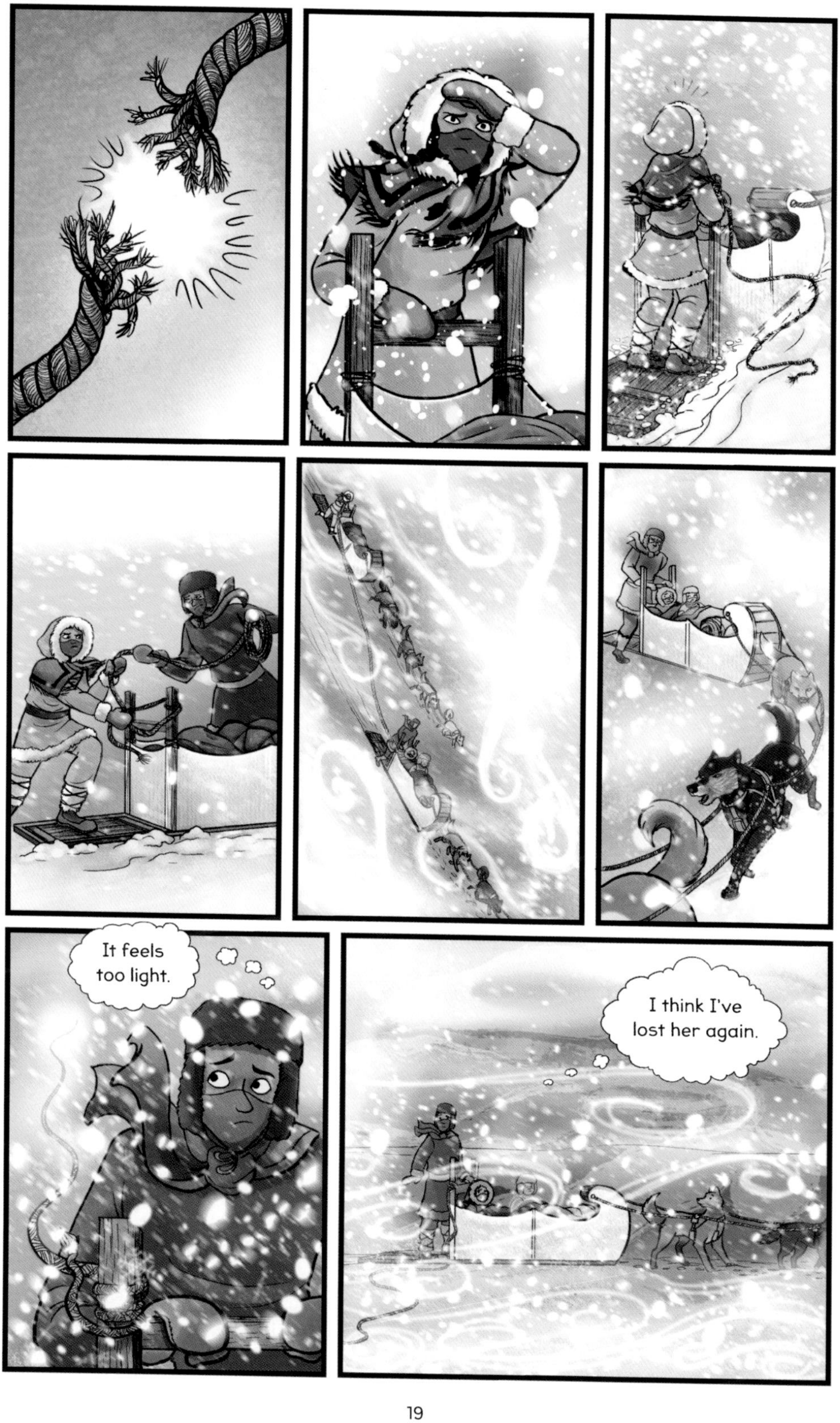
It feels too light.
I think I've lost her again.

It's no use. I've lost him.

I need to control these dogs.

STOP!

phew

Stay warm. Stay calm.

I'll find Windy in the daylight.

Back at Windy Post...

What do you mean she's not with you?

Charles went to Kazan Camp, and we thought we could make it home before the storm.

The storm came so fast. It swallowed us whole.

I tried to keep us together.

I TRIED!

She's still out there.

What should we do?

Mary, get the little boys warm clothes and food and settle them into bed.

It's okay, son.

The northern storms are cruel and can sneak up on even the most seasoned northerner.

Here.

This is where it started to go wrong.

Get some rest. I'll stay up in case she comes back.

We'll radio and head out in the morning.

Fred Schweder, Windy Post. My young daughter is missing in the barren lands. Possibly on Windy River with her dog team. Anyone in the area, please be on the lookout.

DAY 2

Fred Schweder, Windy Post. My young daughter is missing in the barren lands. Again, anyone in the area, please be on the lookout.

The problem was, there was rarely anyone in the area...ever.

Roger that, Mr. Schweder. Our prayers are with you.

Ready? Do you have the pemmican, matches, extra sleeping bags?

Yes. We'll head back to where I think we got separated.

Mary, pay attention to the radio in case we get a call, and look after your brothers while we're gone.

They stayed on a familiar path as long as they could, but the storm hadn't let up, and they could hardly see anything.

Ilse!

Chip!

Blackie!

Chip!

whistle

Here, dogs!

My eyes hurt—I can barely see.

It's been hours now. We have to head home.

I wish we could get a message to Charles so he could look for her on his way back. But there are no radios at camp.

They returned home, hopeful Ilse had somehow found her way back.

Fred Schweder, Windy Post. My daughter is still lost in the Windy or Nueltin area. She is thirteen and without provisions. Over.

Sorry, we didn't find her.

24

Fred catalogued everything Ilse had learned from him and her siblings. They were prepared for life in the north, but being lost in the north was another thing altogether. He was strict, and the children had listened well, but would she remember?

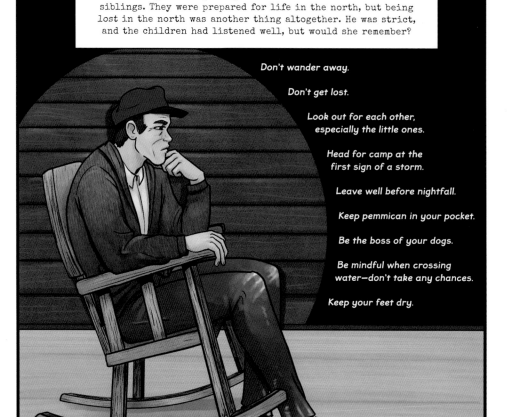

Don't wander away.

Don't get lost.

Look out for each other, especially the little ones.

Head for camp at the first sign of a storm.

Leave well before nightfall.

Keep pemmican in your pocket.

Be the boss of your dogs.

Be mindful when crossing water—don't take any chances.

Keep your feet dry.

Dad, she's smart and careful. She tags along with Charles and me all the time, so she knows a lot.

I was just thinking about Anna.

It's hard to lose a child. I'll never forget when she didn't return home from that...

residential school...

if they want to call it that.

You know, I stopped registering you children as Indian. I thought it might help keep you safe.

I marked your mother as British on your birth certificates.

That was a good idea, Dad.

Let's have tea and get some sleep. I'm ready to look for Ilse again tomorrow.

I'll put the cold tea bags on my eyes. That helps with snow blindness.

Chapter Six: Just the Beginning

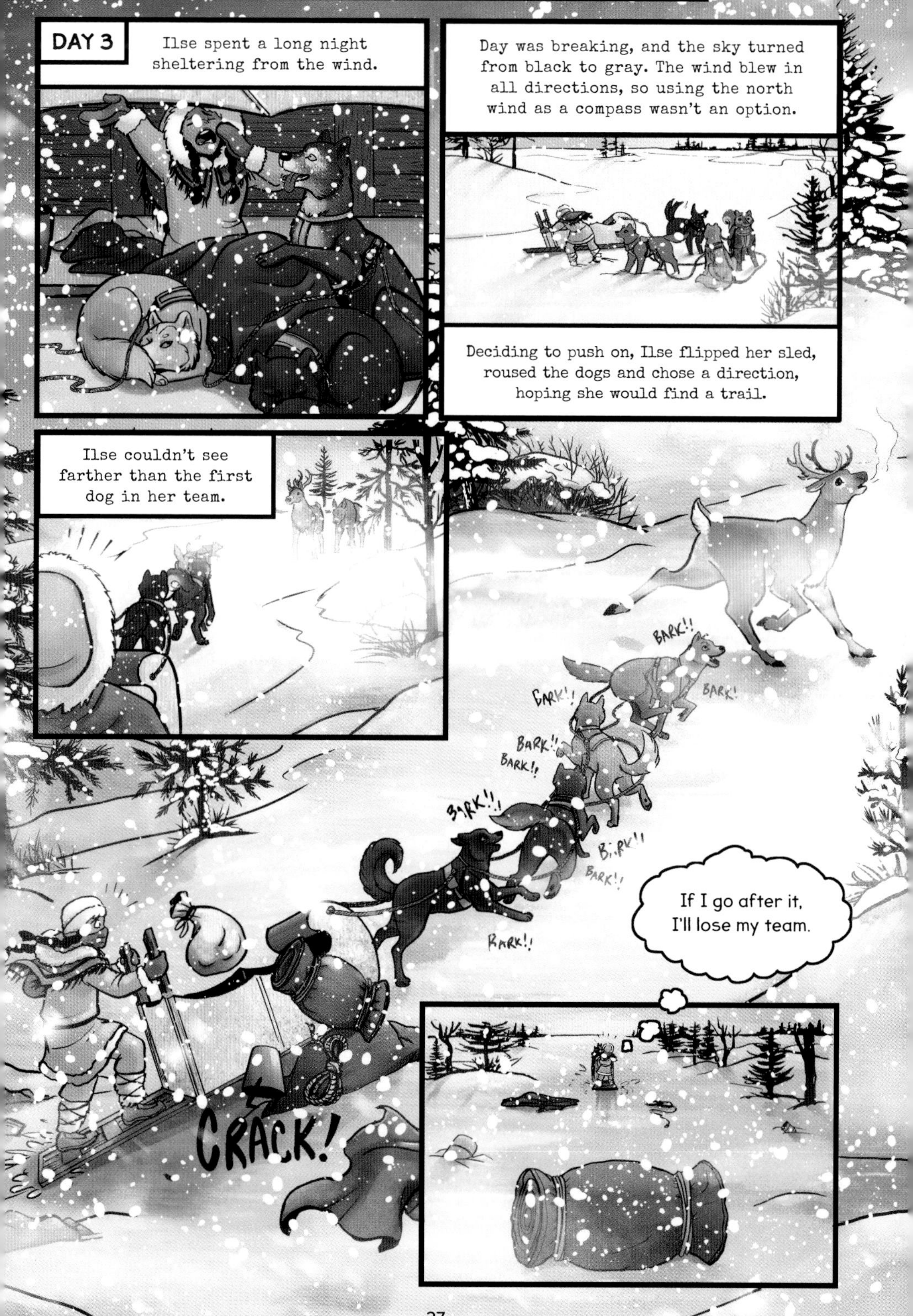
DAY 3
Ilse spent a long night sheltering from the wind.
Day was breaking, and the sky turned from black to gray. The wind blew in all directions, so using the north wind as a compass wasn't an option.
Deciding to push on, Ilse flipped her sled, roused the dogs and chose a direction, hoping she would find a trail.
Ilse couldn't see farther than the first dog in her team.
BARK!!
BARK!
BARK!!
BARK!!
BARK!!
BARK!!
BARK!!
BARK!!
BARK!!
BARK!!
If I go after it, I'll lose my team.
CRACK!

No supplies.

Of course Fred has all of it because his dogs are stronger.

Pemmican. Please be here.

Ilse was just beginning to realize how hungry and thirsty she was. She thought of home, of pemmican, as she drifted off to sleep.

Pemmican is from the Cree word *pimîhkân*—the first part of the word, *pimiy*, means "fat" or "grease." It is made from dried meat crushed into powder using a special tool. The powder is then mixed with fat and formed into bars. Pemmican lasts for years and is a staple food of northerners.

Ilse wasn't sure how long she slept.

After waking up, she continued on her sled.

Ouch! I've cut myself.

My nails are coming off too.

SLURP!

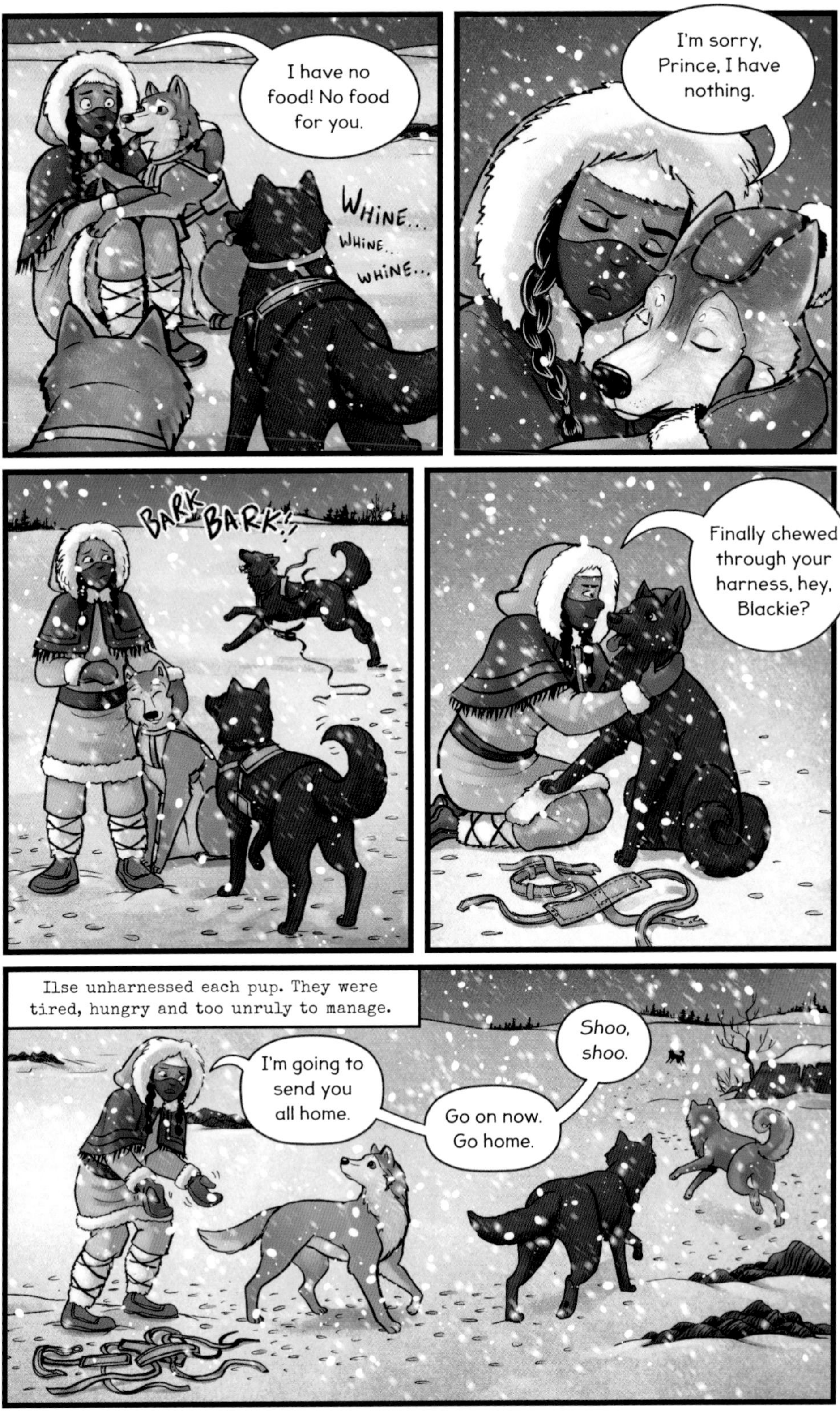
I have no food! No food for you.
WHINE... WHINE... WHINE...
I'm sorry, Prince, I have nothing.
BARK BARK!
Finally chewed through your harness, hey, Blackie?
Ilse unharnessed each pup. They were tired, hungry and too unruly to manage.
I'm going to send you all home.
Go on now. Go home.
Shoo, shoo.

Ilse thought about running after them, in case they knew the way, but decided not to.

She hoped some of the pups would find their way home. Without any food, they would surely die if they stayed with her.

Setting them free was their best chance of survival.

Now I'm really alone.

Her sore, bruised hands and torn fingernails could no longer hold the reins to drive the sled anyway.

I'll come back for the sled once I'm home and rested.

Ilse figured she had spent two nights in the elements so far.

She warmed water by melting scoops of snow in her hands, so her body wouldn't get even colder when she drank it.

Walk, rest, drink...

Spotting higher ground, Ilse went there to look for clues to her location, but nothing gave her any sense of where she was.

Feeling tired, Ilse built a snow cave for shelter that night, digging first with her hands and then with a rock when her hands could no longer dig.

You're lost.

No, I'm not.

Don't worry— just get some sleep.

A winter survival tactic is to build a **snow cave** out of a drift of hard-packed, crusty snow. You can dig into the snow beneath to carve out a space that fits a person. The snow is insulating and provides warmth and shelter from the wind.

Ilse woke up hungry and stiff. The March nights were cold once the sun went down, and she decided it was no longer safe to sleep at night. She would sleep in the daytime, when it was warmer, and keep her body moving during the night.

Show me a clue that will guide me home. A sled track, herd tracks, anything.

A stone man, an inukshuk, a camp.

I wish I had learned more about stars and wayfinding.

Thank you for your light, tipiskâwi-pîsim.

tipiskâwi-pîsim is a **Cree spirit** who is the caretaker of the moon. She keeps the fire going that lights the moon. Her brother, pîsim, does the same for the sun.

Ilse scanned the sky for flares her family might be sending up to help her find her way.

Last Christmas Charles sent up flares as fireworks to entertain the kids.

Everyone, dinner is ready!

Stuffed chickens, fresh bread, apple pie, custard pie, ribbon candy.

What a feast!

Find some music on the radio, Freddy.

Dad, if we move south one day, we can have a tree with branches on both sides.

These poor northern trees have branches on only one side.

sigh...

Day was breaking, and Ilse was tired of walking. She kept her mind occupied with thoughts of home, humming a traditional fiddle tune called "Red River Jig."

Okay, I need to stay organized.

Shelter, keep my clothes dry, water, food...

Oh, I wish I had some food.

RUSTLE
RUSTLE

Please be Chip.

Just breathe.

Ilse had seen many wolves before, but she'd had her dogs for protection, or her father would fire a shot into the air, sending the wolves running.

Both Ilse and the wolf were still, the only movement the tiny puffs of breath that froze and floated away in front of their faces.

Needing to break the silence of the standoff, Ilse said the first thing that came to her mind.

Boo!

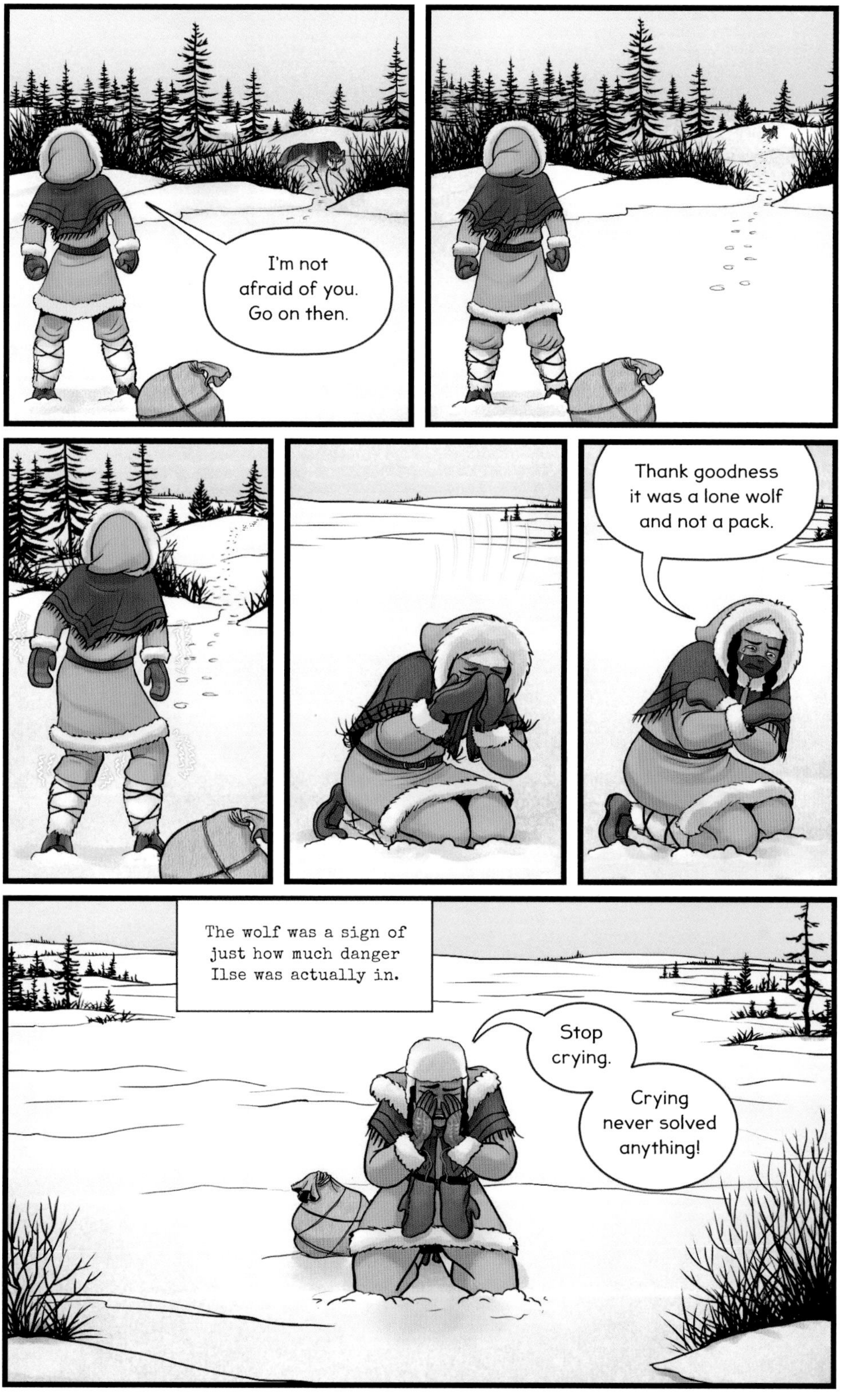
I'm not afraid of you. Go on then.
Thank goodness it was a lone wolf and not a pack.
The wolf was a sign of just how much danger Ilse was actually in.
Stop crying.
Crying never solved anything!

Ilse followed the wolf's path to the top of a ridge to make sure it was gone.

Just like Dad's chart.

Middle claws straight, flanks curved.

One, two, three, four full claw impressions—

fully defined prints.

It reminded her of her dad's drawing, when she was learning to trap,

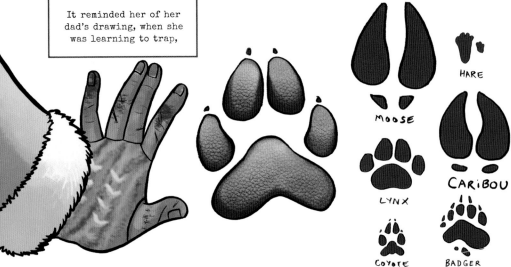

HARE

MOOSE

CARIBOU

LYNX

COYOTE

BADGER

and also of a prized piece of beadwork that had belonged to her mother, whose family was of the Wolf Clan.

Maybe that was why the wolf had walked away from her, leaving her unharmed.

Just a visit from an ancestor—after all, the wolf represents loyalty, protection and family ties.

Spruce sap!

It wasn't much, but she knew she needed to eat something.

She wished for a break from the wind that whistled across the barren land. Her ears ached from it.

Mom always said that if you listen closely you can hear the voices of your ancestors riding on the wind.

KEEP GOING, GRANDDAUGHTER.

Chapter Eight: atihk (Caribou)

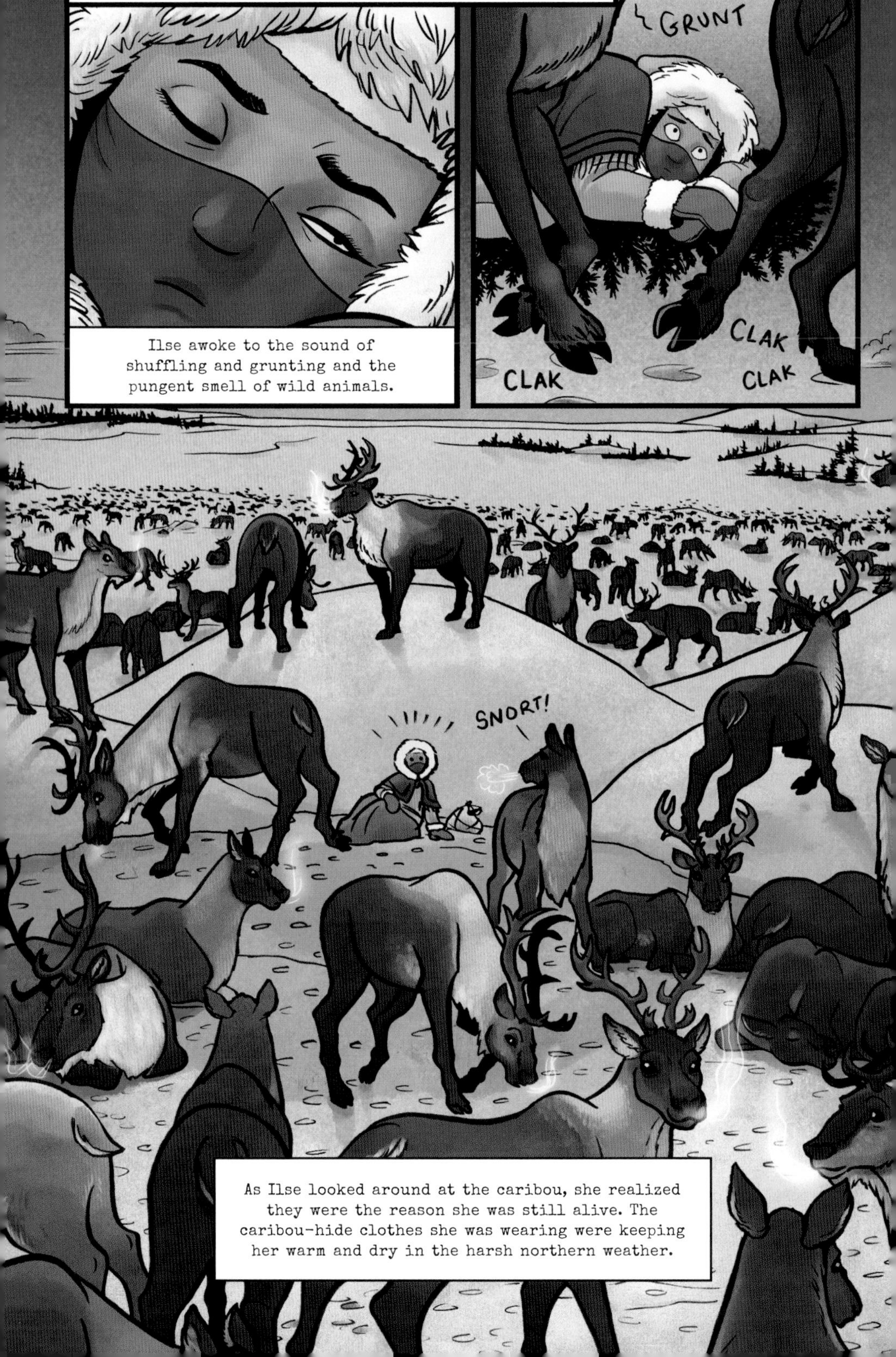
Ilse awoke to the sound of shuffling and grunting and the pungent smell of wild animals.
GRUNT
CLAK
CLAK
CLAK
SNORT!
As Ilse looked around at the caribou, she realized they were the reason she was still alive. The caribou-hide clothes she was wearing were keeping her warm and dry in the harsh northern weather.

Their antlers are starting to drop.

Spring is coming.

Maybe my ancestors sent them after all.

Ilse lay there unafraid, as atihk were longtime friends of her people. It was believed they had sacrificed themselves to ensure the survival of the tribes.

Find your instincts.

You're on the right path.

atihk's Gifts

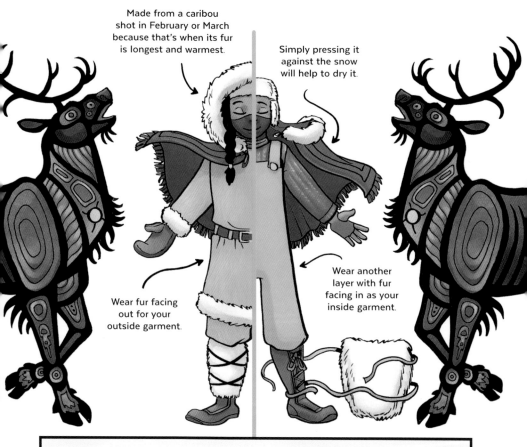

Made from a caribou shot in February or March because that's when its fur is longest and warmest.

Simply pressing it against the snow will help to dry it.

Wear fur facing out for your outside garment.

Wear another layer with fur facing in as your inside garment.

From **caribou** we learn that family comes first. They walk some 3,100 miles (5,000 kilometers) each year to find a safe place to have their young. No map, just their instincts to guide the massive herds. A traditional belief is that seeing a caribou is a sign you're on the right path.

Ilse slept soundly among the herd, as she knew *exactly* where the caribou were going. They were headed north to have their young, which meant she now knew which direction was which.

DAY 6

Ennadia Lake...

Sand Hill Camp...

Windy?

Her brother Charles was an expert mapmaker, and she had studied his work.

She knew the twists and turns of the trapline path, but the body of water she was walking beside confused her.

She didn't know which side she was on. She might have crossed water unknowingly during the storm.

Southeast. It's backtracking, but it makes the most sense.

I'll either hit a camp on the trapline or, hopefully, home.

Ilse wanted to be angry that she was headed back the way she had come, but she took a deep breath and walked down the path the caribou had beaten.

On the lookout for more landmarks, Ilse spotted an inukshuk in the distance.

Ilse and her brothers had built an inukshuk once, although it wasn't as grand as this one.

Their inukshuk marked a place that was abundant with fish—they had caught a magnificent lake trout there.

It might have been the biggest on record, but no one would ever know because they'd eaten it for supper.

Inukshuks are an ancient method of communication. They are stacks of stones that can be found throughout the north. They can signal a good fishing spot, communicate direction or even give a warning.

She started across the crusty snow toward the inukshuk.

Oh no!

KRAK!! KRAK!!

Ahhhhh!

KRAK!!

SPLASH

Gasp!

It's freezing!

Ilse quickly started to gather spruce branches to lay her wet garments on and give her something to stand on.

I have to get my mukluks and socks off fast.

Ilse flipped her mukluks inside out and pressed the fur against the snow. The snow sucked up the water from the fur, drying them.

If only my wool socks could do that.

Frostbite... it's starting.

My feet ache so bad!

She wedged herself into the low branches of the spruce tree, put her mitts over her toes and went to sleep.

Chapter Nine: wapihiw (Willow Ptarmigan)

DAY 7

Oh no! My eyes are starting to get scratchy, and things look blurry.

I hope it's not the start of snow blindness.

Snow blindness is a sunburn on the eyes caused by the glare of the sun reflected off the white snow. It causes blurred vision and feels like you've had sand thrown in your eyes. It's very painful. Ilse had had it before and remembered lying in bed with cold tea bags over her eyes. The Inuit used to make **snow goggles** from wood or bone, with tiny slits to protect their eyes from snow blindness.

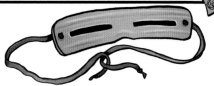

I have to deal with this before it gets worse.

Riiiiiiiiiiip...

JAB
JAB
JAB

There.

I don't have goggles, so this will have to do.

From her cold, aching feet to her itchy eyes to the throbbing cut on her hand, physical injuries were starting to take their toll on Ilse. Her growling stomach was a constant reminder that there was no food to be had.

As she walked and looked through the tiny hole, something caught Ilse's eye.

It was a fox den...

That looks like willow ptarmigan feathers.

There are chickens nearby!

Am I imagining this?

PiP!

PiP!

PiP!

KUK-KUK-KUK

PiP!

KUK-KUK

YES!

Willow ptarmigan are a symbol of a mother's love, determination and sacrifice, as they're known to be brave protectors of their young. They use deception to lead prey from their nest, often losing their own lives as a result. Because they don't migrate south, they were a staple food at the Windy Post year-round. Ilse's family called them chickens. Their sound was annoyingly loud, and Ilse and her brothers often threw rocks to shoo them away from the cabin.

Ilse's heart raced, and her feet moved faster than they had all day. The willow ptarmigan were surely feeding, and if her instincts were correct, they would lead her to a patch of cranberry shrubs lying hidden under the snow.

I have to look carefully to be sure.

I'll taste just one, and then I'll know.

It's a cranberry, all right.

Ow ow ow!

My fingers hurt, but I need as many as I can get.

DIG... DIG... DIG...

Ilse ate a few handfuls of berries as she dug, but then she stopped. She was feeling queasy, as she hadn't eaten in a few days.

Thank you, chickens.

Thank you so much for leading me here.

Standing up and turning, Ilse saw two grave markers in the snow behind her.

I wonder who they are.

Dene?

Cree?

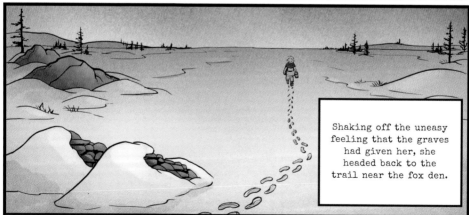

Shaking off the uneasy feeling that the graves had given her, she headed back to the trail near the fox den.

There used to be many grave sites like this throughout the north. You couldn't bury people because it wasn't easy to dig through the **permafrost**.

Maybe I can "neak" up on it.

HA HAH HA!

It was a reference to an old family joke.

How do you catch a unique rabbit?

How?

You "neak" up on it!

haha!

How do you catch a tame rabbit?

How?

The "tame" way.

With cranberries in her stomach, a smirk on her face from the rabbit joke, and the weight of the full tea pail on her arm, Ilse felt a lift in her spirit and a will to continue.

I believe it won't be long until someone finds me.

Mangiggal.

That's what the Inuit call this type of snow.

Inuit have many words to describe snow. When something can affect your daily life based on its state, there must be a way to speak of it.

Aqilokoq	Softly falling snow
Piqsirpoq	Drifting snow
Pukak	Snow that has the consistency of salt
Mangiggal	Hard snow with a crusted top

It is so hard-packed with a polished surface that sleds and footprints barely leave a mark.

It makes it hard to see Ilse's tracks.

There are two times a day when we can look for Ilse.

The sun has to be flat with the horizon so we can see marks in the snow.

We've been spreading out and looking, but we're only finding small clues to the trails she might have taken.

And the storm blew snow over any tracks she did leave.

After sunset Charles returned home with news that he'd found tracks, but they appeared to show Ilse on the wrong path.

She seems to be headed away from the camp, but she's off the trapline.

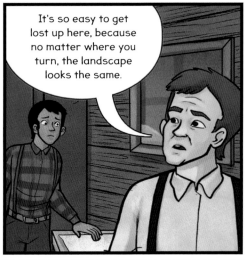

It's so easy to get lost up here, because no matter where you turn, the landscape looks the same.

I've always told you kids that if you get lost, you'll never find your way.

I sure hope I'm wrong.

We'll get some rest and then head out to meet the sunrise near the tracks I saw and follow them from there.

Northern lights can be bright green, pink or even purple. Ilse's Cree mother told her they were ancestors trying to get your attention. The Inuit say they are the spirits of the dead playing ball with a walrus skull. Her brothers used to say that if you whistled loudly they would come down and steal you. That never failed to send the children running and screaming back into the cabin.

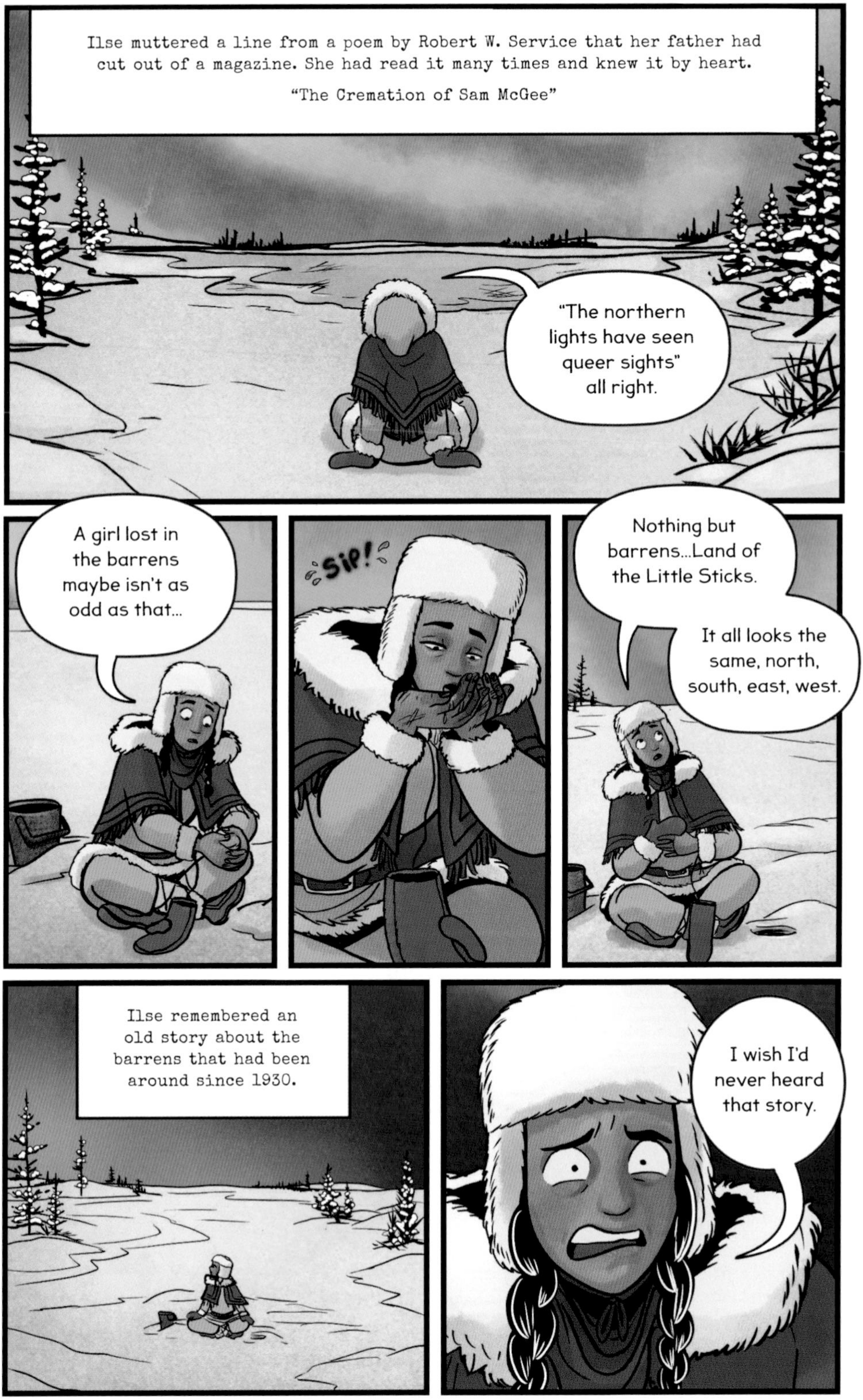
Ilse muttered a line from a poem by Robert W. Service that her father had cut out of a magazine. She had read it many times and knew it by heart.
"The Cremation of Sam McGee"
"The northern lights have seen queer sights" all right.
A girl lost in the barrens maybe isn't as odd as that...
SIP!
Nothing but barrens...Land of the Little Sticks.
It all looks the same, north, south, east, west.
Ilse remembered an old story about the barrens that had been around since 1930.
I wish I'd never heard that story.

A trapper named Joe Labelle was traveling near Lake Angikuni.

Cold and tired from walking, he headed to a fishing village he knew was friendly to visitors.

Walking into camp, he saw a fire that still had burning embers.

A pot of stew hung over it was burned to a crisp.

He popped his head into each of the six tents and found no one, just abandoned tasks, rifles and supplies.

He searched the outskirts of the village for tracks and saw none.

Stranger still, he found a group of hungry sled dogs and an unearthed grave with the body removed.

He was spooked. And although he needed rest, his feet kept him moving through the night.

Joe made his way to the nearest telegraph station and reported what he'd seen to the RCMP.

THE NORTH TIMES

MYSTERIOUS HAPPENIN AT ANGIKUNI LAKE
RCMP ARE BAFFLED BY THE DISAPPEARANCE

ARCTIC TELEC

GAZETTE

RANGE LIGHTS N THE NORTH

There were theories about UFOs and alien abductions as RCMP investigators heard reports of strange blue lights in the sky.

Yet others believed it to be the work of Torngaruk, a powerful, mischievous sky deity visible only to Inuit shamans.

In the end no one found out what had happened, and none of the villagers were ever seen again.

Use Mary's mind trick. Tuck it away.

Put the scary thought in an envelope and mail it far away.

I'm sending it to Greenland!

This snow cave was a little smaller and less comfortable than the last. Her body was weaker, her clothes baggier and her mind fuzzier.

Ilse fell asleep thinking about her family's lives as fur traders. It was hard to believe that they lived this life for the sake of fashion.

The **fur trade** began on the east coast of Canada in the 16th century. As demand for furs grew, companies such as the Hudson's Bay Company established trading posts across the country, including the far north. One of the most valuable trade items were beaver pelts. They were turned into top hats for men across Europe. Trappers and fur traders were adventurous men, fit, rough and resourceful. In the north they caught foxes and other animals, baling the furs and transporting them away to become coats, hats and shawls. In Canada in 1944, 100,000 women purchased fur coats.

"This is the life - no worries, taxes or traffic.
I'm free to do as I like."
- Ragnar Jonsson

Ragnar Jonsson was a Swedish-born master trapper who made his way to Canada in 1923.

He worked as a fisher, woodcutter and railroad laborer before turning to trapping.

He found his true home in the Canadian north and was known as one of the most skilled outdoorsmen working on the Manitoba-Northwest Territories border.

Ragnar's home base was on the island that bears his name, Jonsson Island.

Ragnar had an oil lamp, some sleeping bags and a woodstove made from an oil drum.

His house was a tepee-like structure made of tin. Although he could have built a cabin, he didn't want to waste that much wood.

He had a supply of macaroni, flour, beans, sugar, coffee and tea. He also had stacks of *TIME* magazine that he'd picked up when he occasionally traveled to Churchill, Manitoba, to collect his mail.

He lived almost completely off the land.

Once he went two years without speaking to another human.

The Schweders had traded with him many times.

He was an honest and trustworthy man, so much so that trading-post managers would accept checks from him that were just notes written on old paper bags.

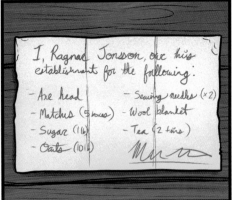

I, Ragnar Jonsson, owe this establishment for the following:
- Axe head
- Matches (5 boxes)
- Sugar (1 lb)
- Oats (10 lb)
- Sewing needles (x2)
- Wool blanket
- Tea (2 tins)

It had been nine days since Ilse was separated from her brothers, but she had lost track of how much time had passed.

I'm so tired. I miss my family.

My feet hurt so much.

Ilse thought the land around her was starting to look familiar. She didn't know it yet, but she was trekking toward Jonsson Island in Nueltin Lake, also known as Sleeping Island, its traditional Dene name.

I need to find Ragnar's place.

I need to find the high rock.

Get up. He's close to here—

I know it.

Those must be Ragnar's. Thank you!

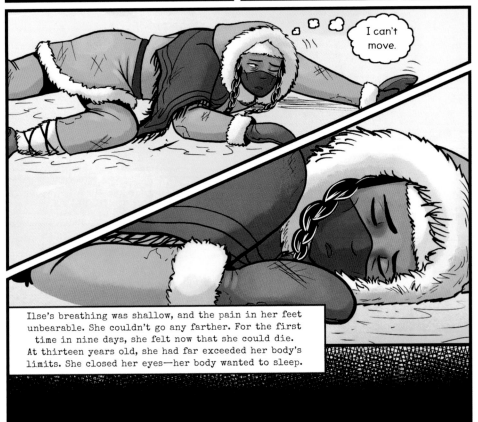

Ilse's breathing was shallow, and the pain in her feet unbearable. She couldn't go any farther. For the first time in nine days, she felt now that she could die. At thirteen years old, she had far exceeded her body's limits. She closed her eyes—her body wanted to sleep.

Chapter Twelve: Contact

BANG!!

Is this real?

Don't shoot.

Please.

Who are you?

I'm Ilse Schweder.

Yes, Schweder. But what are you doing here?

Where's your dad? Where is Charles?

I got lost in the storm about a week ago, and I've been trying to walk home ever since.

Okay, we need to get you inside. My camp is just up the hill. Can you make it?

No, I don't think so.

My feet are hurting, and I'm so tired.

Okay, Ilse, don't worry. I'll bring a tent down to you.

Are you hungry?

No.

Ragnar hauled everything from his camp by dogsled.

He set up a tent around Ilse and made tea.

Ragnar took off her frozen mukluks to dry and warm by the fire and covered her with several blankets.

You have to try to drink.

Okay, I'll try.

Ilse sipped on the tea, feeling it warm her empty insides.

Can you eat? I have a boiled caribou tongue.

No, I'm going to sleep.

Ragnar kept the fire and the tea going all night, tending to Ilse and making plans.

Okay, Ilse. I've made some caribou-blood pancakes. Eat a little, okay?

Okay. Thank you.

Ilse, do you think you know your way home from here? I might need your help.

I think so. Now that I'm here, I have some sense of direction back.

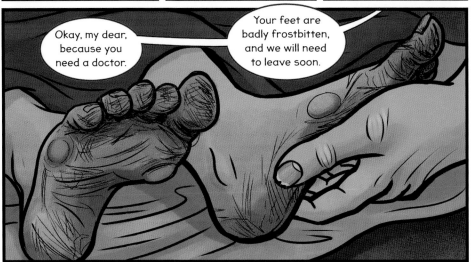

Okay, my dear, because you need a doctor.

Your feet are badly frostbitten, and we will need to leave soon.

I'll prepare a sled. You rest and eat until I'm ready, Ilse.

Home...

Your family must be worried, so best we start now.

Ragnar placed Ilse in the cariole and covered her in blankets.

He traveled all day and night. He woke her once in a while to help with wayfinding.

Ilse, does this look right?

I made it. I made it.

Ilse, I'll go in to get help to carry you.

One minute now.

Hello!

Hello...

There was no one there, but the stove was lit, so they couldn't be far away.

They aren't here. I'll help you inside. Lean on me.

My feet...

Ilse felt the rush of warm air on her face and smelled freshly baked bread.

There's a note here, Ilse. They are out looking for you near the old Hudson's Bay post where they last spotted some tracks.

I won't leave until your family is back.

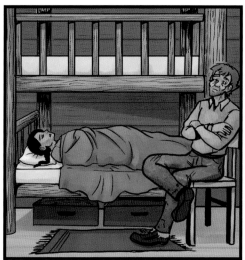

They're back.

BARK! BARK!

OH, ILSE!

You look so thin!

I'm so glad to be home. I'm so happy Ragnar found me.

Well, I think you found me, actually.

How are you feeling?

I'm not doing so well. My feet really hurt.

We've been looking every day, sister.

We found some of your dogs yesterday.

Dad and everyone else should be here soon.

KIDS,
ILSE'S HOME!
COME QUICK!

What happened?

Were you scared?

Where did you sleep?

Oh, Ilse, I'm so happy to see you. You're one lucky girl.

We looked every day for you, my girl. Following the most crooked trail we've ever seen.

SKELETON LAKE

SAND HILL CAMP

NORTH CAMP

HOME

LOST!

SPRUCE CAMP

GEORGE!

WINDY RIVER

LOON LAKE

RAGNAR'S ISLAND

Some of those lakes you crossed, you could have fallen through the ice!

I did once...

I'm sorry. I'm so sorry I lost you.

It wasn't your fault. That storm sure snuck up quick.

Uh, Fred. Look at her feet. She needs to see a doctor very soon.

Mary, boil some water and help Ilse get cleaned up.

We need to soak her feet in very hot water.

It stung so badly to plunge her feet into the hot water. Mary added iodine to help.

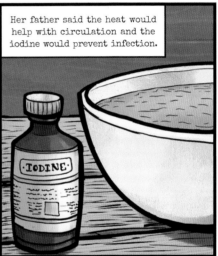

Her father said the heat would help with circulation and the iodine would prevent infection.

IODINE

While Ilse slept, finally in the comfort of her home, the family quietly had dinner with Ragnar.

Thank you, Ragnar, thank you so much.

To Ragnar.

To Ragnar.

Mary, tend to your sister through the night. Make sure she drinks a lot and that you keep her cuts clean.

NOD NOD NOD

Ragnar, you can stay here tonight. There is a room in the trapper's hut.

Thank you, I will.

Even though Ilse needed rest, Fred had decided she needed a doctor as soon as they could be ready to leave.

We need to take her to Brochet, so let's get some rest.

It could take three or four days depending on how much open water we see.

So let's start preparing.

The next morning Ragnar packed for the journey home. The family gave him pemmican, two frozen berry pies and a loaf of bread.

Thank you again, Ragnar.

The family will be forever grateful to you.

Chapter Thirteen: Brochet

Travel to Brochet is going to be challenging at this time of year.

Some lakes will be partially frozen, but there will be open water too.

We'll have to put Ilse and the supplies in a canoe, and the dogs can pull it. When we hit open water we'll all have to canoe until the ice is solid again.

I radioed ahead, so the doctor will be waiting.

They traveled along the ice, and when a spot wasn't crossable, the canoe would float and the dogs would have to plunge into the icy water and swim...

...sometimes scared into the task by a gun being fired into the air.

WINDY RIVER

NUELTIN LAKE

FORT HALL

LAC BROCHET

KAPUSKAYPACHIK

WOLLASTON LAKE

BROCHET

REINDEER LAKE

How long were you out there, Ilse?

A week maybe?

It was nine days, doctor.

Extraordinary that you are doing this well, young lady.

May I speak with you in private?

Of course.

It's frostbite to the worst possible degree, I'm afraid.

I think she needs to go to a surgical hospital where they can amputate her feet.

I'm so sorry.

Is that necessary?

The risk of infection is great. If it sets in, it will overtake her, and you'll be too far away to get any emergency treatment.

She'll stay in the infirmary and take penicillin. The antibiotics will start to help her while you decide.

Thank you.

You've given me a lot to consider. I'm going to get some advice.

The doctor wants to amputate her feet, but I don't know.

It's risky to treat frozen feet, but I have seen people heal.

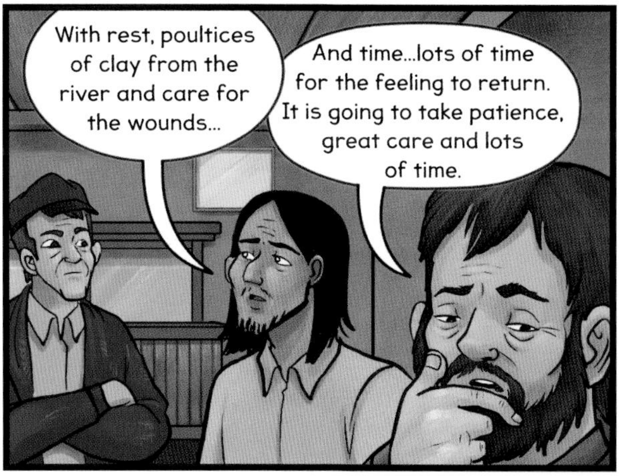
With rest, poultices of clay from the river and care for the wounds...
And time...lots of time for the feeling to return. It is going to take patience, great care and lots of time.

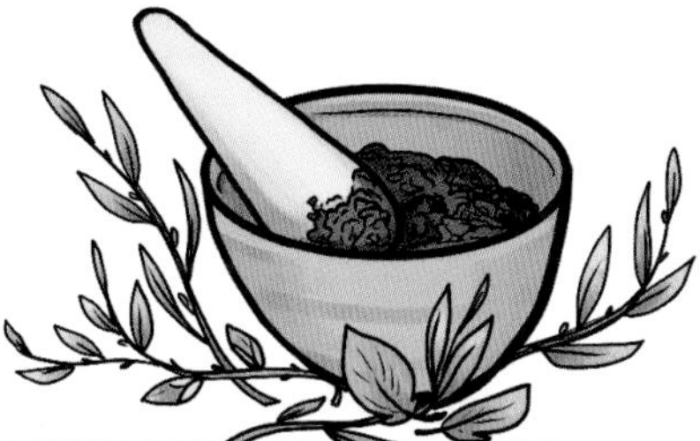

A **poultice** is a traditional way of treating inflammation, infections and other ailments. It is a homemade paste that might contain clay, flour, baking soda and herbs. The paste is spread directly on the body or onto a warm cloth laid over the area.

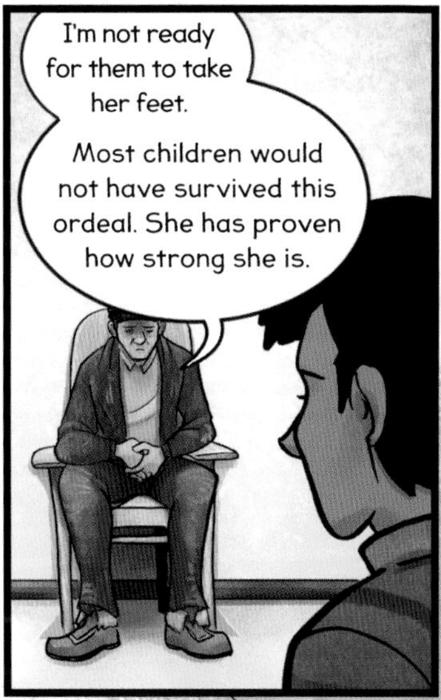
I'm not ready for them to take her feet.
Most children would not have survived this ordeal. She has proven how strong she is.

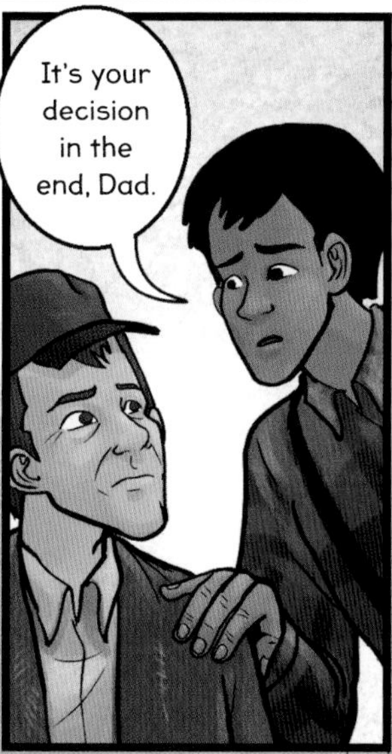
It's your decision in the end, Dad.

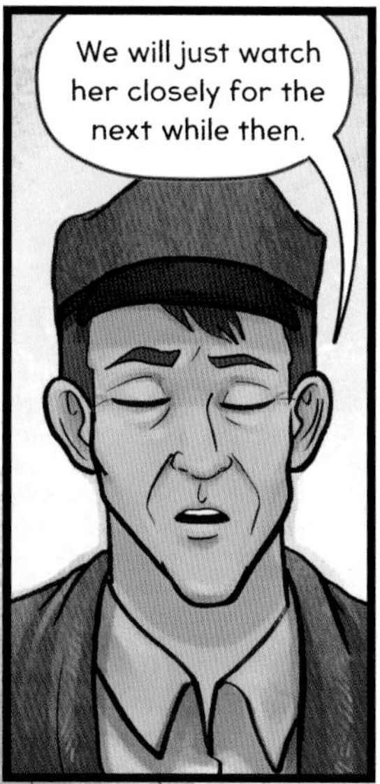
We will just watch her closely for the next while then.

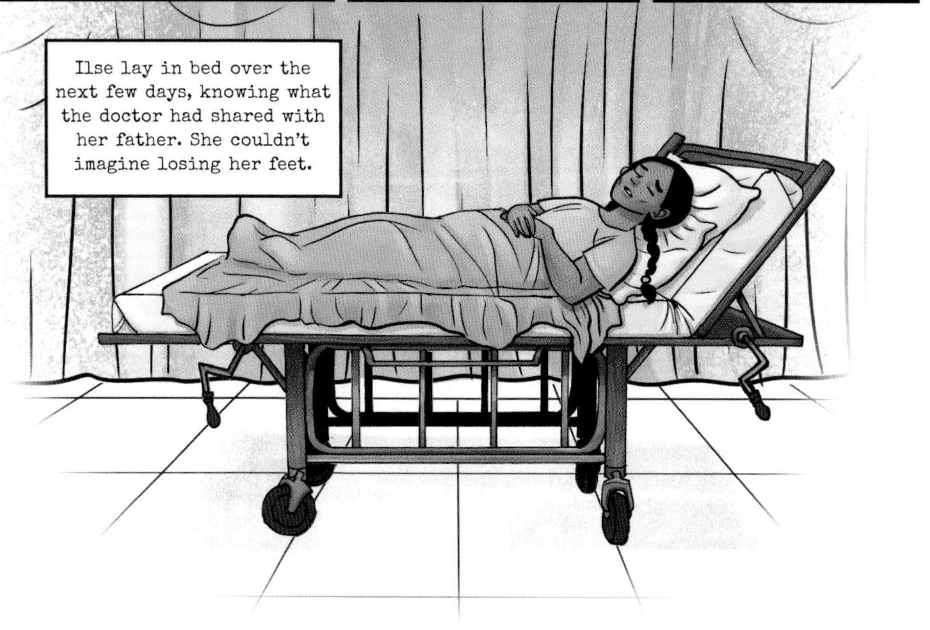
Ilse lay in bed over the next few days, knowing what the doctor had shared with her father. She couldn't imagine losing her feet.

If you say so, Mr. Schweder. I'll say it again. This is against my advice, but I'll write you some instructions.

I'll also give you some antibiotics and something to help with her pain. She will be in a lot of pain as her feet recover.

Okay, thank you. I do know it's a risk, but I think her equal to the task.

When will we leave?

Two more days under the doctor's care.

If the infection is under control we can use traditional medicine at home.

We'll stock up on supplies since we're here...

And Dad, I think you've made the right choice.

Ilse sobbed tears of joy when her father broke the news. Other than her feet, she was doing surprisingly well. The road ahead would be difficult, but amputation was an alternative they were not ready to face.

Chapter Fourteen: The Road to Recovery

As expected, the following months were difficult for Ilse. When the rivers and lakes unfroze, the family made thick poultices of clay and herbs and applied them to her feet.

Any new feeling today?

Just the shooting pain. I still can't feel those three toes.

And your bedsores.

My whole body hurts. I want to move, but I can't.

Okay, sit up. Time to move your ankles and knees like Dad said.

All right then.

These movements will help when you're finally ready to walk again.

Let's go.

It would be seven months until Ilse was able to walk again. She walked slowly at first but got stronger every day.

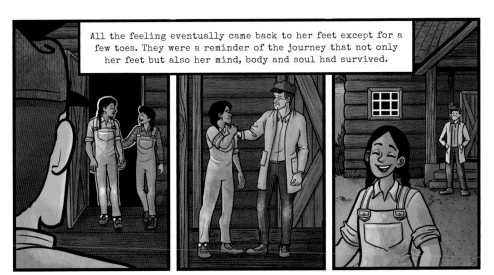

All the feeling eventually came back to her feet except for a few toes. They were a reminder of the journey that not only her feet but also her mind, body and soul had survived.

In the years to come, people in the north would ask her to tell the story about getting lost in the barrens. She told them the caribou were her guides.

Their hides kept her warm, the animals showed her where to walk and they even surrounded her and kept her safe one night. From that day forward, when the herds thundered past the post, she would close her eyes and thank them with a prayer.

Chapter Fifteen: Reclaimed

And that's what really happened.

That's why I say that Stella couldn't have done what I did. She didn't know the things I knew.

Old Mowat's Stella wouldn't have lasted the night.

!HA HA HA!

!HA HA HA!

What I didn't know as a girl was all life was preparation.

The Creator wanted me to endure this.

It's our experiences, you see. All these things that we've seen, done, achieved and lived through make us who we are.

Some of these things may be difficult, like losing my mother at such a young age or being taken away to residential school.

But some experiences are joyful. Together they all add up to knowledge, strength and perspective.

You might not realize it now, but there's a lesson inside every moment.

When you leave here today, pay attention to your surroundings. Look and listen more closely.

Open your eyes and mind up wide. Watch and learn from your elders, from nature and even animals.

I want to be like you! A strong survivor.

Well then, you've got to make sure you can think for yourself.

In those days we had to figure things out ourselves or speak to someone who could teach us.

Would you ever go back there?

I'd live up there forever if I could. And you know, it really is a beautiful land.

If you get a chance to go up north, you should take it.

When I was young it felt as if only Indigenous people, such as the Inuit, Chipweyan and Cree—and later, curious explorers and fur traders—had ever roamed this part of Canada.

Those who've made the trip and those who made a life there in the north know a secret.

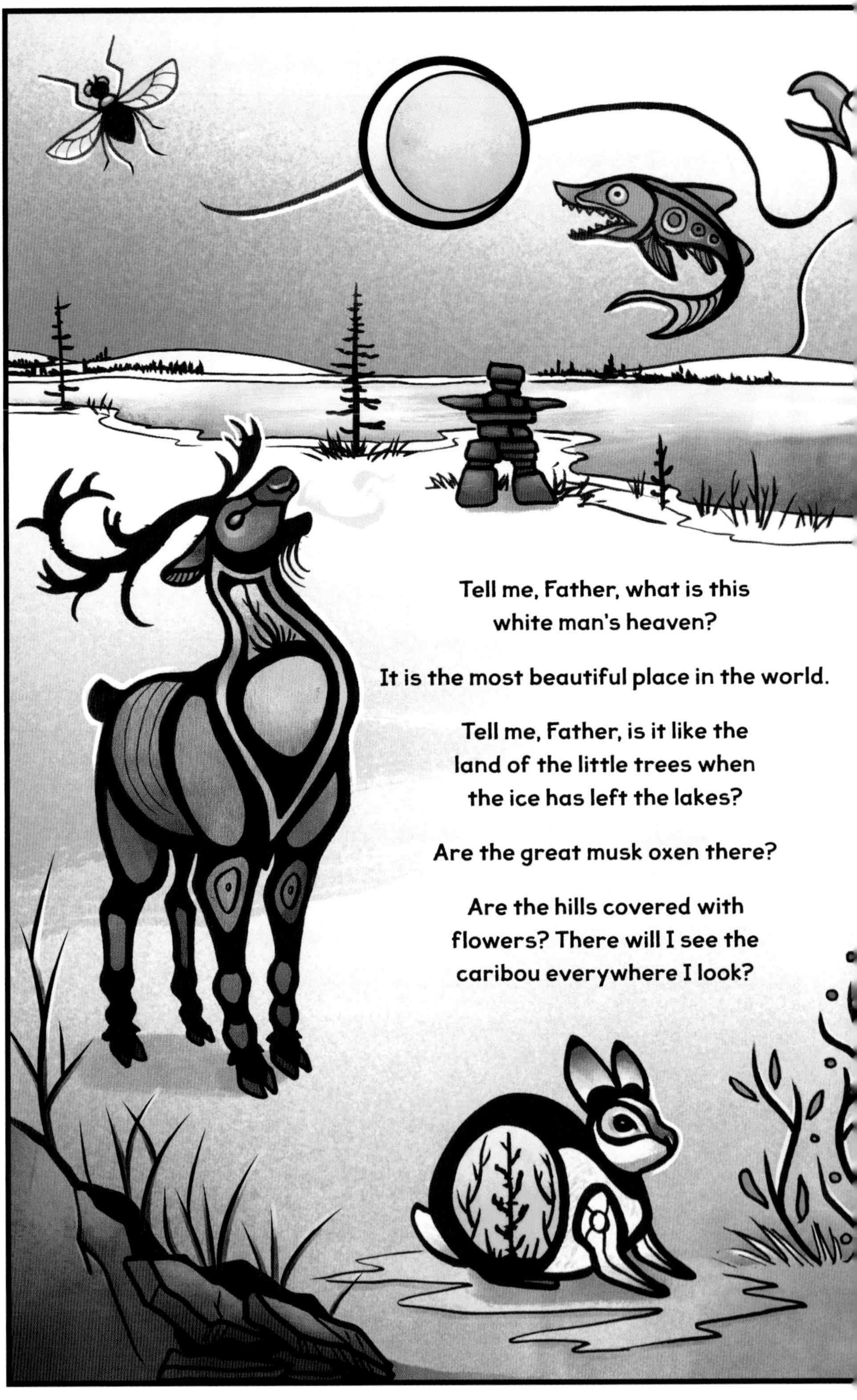

Tell me, Father, what is this
white man's heaven?

It is the most beautiful place in the world.

Tell me, Father, is it like the
land of the little trees when
the ice has left the lakes?

Are the great musk oxen there?

Are the hills covered with
flowers? There will I see the
caribou everywhere I look?

Are the lakes blue with
the sky of summer?

Is every net full of great, fat whitefish?

Is there room for me in this land,
like our land, the Barrens?

Can I camp anywhere and not find
that someone else has camped?

Can I feel the wind and be like the wind?

Father, if your heaven is not
all these, leave me alone in my
land of the little sticks.

—Dialogue between an Indigenous man
and a priest recorded by Warburton
Pike in *The Barren Ground of Northern
Canada* published in 1892.

Ilse at the long-abandoned Windy Post.

Rosa Bighetty and her children traveling by train to Churchill.

Ilse as a teenager in Churchill, Manitoba.

Cabin at the Windy Post insulated with snow.

Sled dogs along a winter road.

Ilse visiting Ragnar at his campsite.

Trapper still recalls saving woman's life

THOMPSON, Man. (CP) — Thirty-seven years ago, Elsie Bruderer was lost in the remote north and near death after spending nine days without food.

Bruderer and her two brothers had been driving dog teams in the family trading post, but she became separated from her brothers in a snow storm.

Her dog team, now starving, became unmanageable so she left the dogs and continued her search on foot. Eventually, she fell asleep in the snow.

That was where she was found by Ragnar Jonsson, a Swedish-born rugged trapper who has been living alone in Manitoba's remote north since 1938.

Jonsson, who saved Bruderer's life, had first met her five years earlier in 1940, when she was helping her father and brothers trap fur-bearing animals.

"When I looked at those fingers on that day in 1945, they were blue with cold," Jonsson, 82, told Bruderer when the pair had a reunion recently.

"There was no color in the nails and they were broken because you'd had so little food."

Bruderer had been searching for markers around Neultin Lake to give her bearings. One marker was a high rock that turned out to be near Jonsson's cabin.

"I was getting very sick and had a g and greater desire for sleep," she sa Bruderer recalled that Jonsson p tent for her and gave her all the sleeping bags and quilts he had.

"He got me some warm tea, which I could handle at the time."

The next morning, Jonsson put on his dogsled and began a three-d her father's post. Jonsson said h trouble recalling how the young looked then, although 37 years h passed.

"Remember her! I could make of her, but she looks like an oth with her hair all frizzed up."

Bruderer, now a grandmo teaches at a day-care centre in said. "He still remembers me He's an amazing man and I'v such a good friend."

Bruderer was nourished ba with pancakes and tea after J her.

"I still think he could do wi cooking lessons," she said.

Jonsson, who made his first Lake 44 years ago, said he k life of the north, but isn't keeps in touch with world distressed by many current

Photos courtesy of Ilse Schweder.

Author's note

Ilse Schweder was my grandmother. She passed away in 2018 at the age of 87 in Thompson, Manitoba. Her strength and courage are the reasons I'm able to write this today. Ilse had five children and many grandchildren. She taught us all many things, took us camping and fishing, cooked for us, sat and chatted over tea, and much more. Throughout our lives we always heard snippets of the story of when she was lost. Small details here and there, and then she might wrap it up with "Okay, you just never mind then" before moving on.

Someone needs to write her story down was a familiar phrase that echoed in our family for decades. Over coffee one morning, I asked my grandma if I could work with her to write it down, and she accepted. My mother and I visited her and passed her a pouch of tobacco, asking for her blessing. I began by flipping through old photos and asking her lots of questions. I'm glad that I could ask her these questions before she passed away, but I'm sad that she wasn't able to see the book in its published form. How I would have loved for her to do a school visit, toting her own book under her arm.

It had always bothered Ilse that the writer Farley Mowat, who her father met on the train to Churchill, wrote an account of her story in the book *People of the Deer* and made mention of her family in others. He spent time camping outside their trading post too, always scribbling in his notebook. Today Ilse would be happy to know that her story has been reclaimed in a way that was true to her experience.

I remember asking her if she ever thought she was going to die. She said not really, that she was too young to think that way, so she just kept walking. *She just kept walking*—for nine days, at thirteen years old. Only on that very last day, outside Ragnar's home, did she think she might actually die.

In our conversations, she spoke a great deal about the caribou and how they were her guides. They appeared and gave her a sense of direction and even hope. She spoke of the traditional Indigenous knowledge of the land and life in a fur-trading family and how without that understanding, she surely would have perished. Without the physical strength she'd developed from the chores and the lifestyle at the Windy Post, her feet never would have carried her as far as they did. She spoke of having to "think for yourself in those days" and how this made your brain stronger because you couldn't just "look it up."

Ilse loved life in the north—fishing, camping, feeding the animals and being part of a community. She finally did see a wolverine too! My brother and I were going fishing with her and my grandpa Brian in their red camper van, and a wolverine wandered out onto the dirt road. It decided to take on the van, biting the tires and pawing at the door. With no fear, Ilse opened the door to tell it to "shoo," and I can remember Brian yelling, "Close the door, Ilse! Are you crazy?"

"Never mind, I've got this," she said as Brian drove away from the beast.

We miss you so much, Grandma—all of us!

Acknowledgments

In addition to an extensive interview with my grandmother, I did a whole lot of research for this book—in the Hudson's Bay Company archives, on the internet and speaking to family and experts on the history and culture of the day. I even found a letter written by the doctor who had cared for Ilse that referenced her situation. I wanted this story to be how Ilse remembered it but also a teaching tool for young people to learn about life in the north, Indigenous culture and the Schweder family. I received an unexpected gift while sifting through stacks of books, letters, journals and articles—I also learned a lot about my great-grandfather Fred and my great-grandmother Rosa. I almost felt like I had a chance to *meet* them through the research and writing process, and that was very special to me.

We all have someone in our ancestral history who did something great, survived against all odds, faced adversity and won. Someone who did something that ensured their bloodline would move forward, allowing future generations of their family to enjoy life. I encourage you to dive into your own family tree to learn about those who made sure that you are standing here today. For me that person was Ilse, and through writing this book I was able to help build a piece of her legacy and ensure that her memory and story never get lost.

I would like to thank the Canada Council for the Arts for its support of this project. I would also like to thank my friends and family who encouraged me to write this important story, including my husband, Greg, and my son, Owen. They were the official test audiences of my work, allowing me to read all my writing aloud to them. Special thanks to Les Oystryk for sharing his wealth of knowledge and archives, Cara Hedley and Simon Rose for their help with the initial manuscript and Kirstie Hudson for "taking it from there!" as editor. Thank you to the designer, artist and colorist, Dahlia Yuen, Alina Pete and Jillian Dolan respectively, for bringing the pictures to life. And finally, thank you to Orca Book Publishers for their confidence in my work and their belief in the value of sharing my grandmother's story.